Contents

Some words are printed in bold, **like this**. You can find out what they mean in the glossary.

What is Buddhism?

Buddhism began in northern India about 2,500 years ago. A prince, called Siddhartha Gautama, taught people how to overcome suffering and lead happier lives. He became the **Buddha**, "the enlightened one". Buddhists call his teachings the **Dharma**. They use the Dharma as a guide to living their lives in the right manner.

From India, Buddhism spread to other parts of Asia and beyond. Today, it is one of the major religions with some 400 million followers around the world.

Beliefs and practice

Among the world's religions, Buddhism is unusual because it is not based on a belief in a divine being called God. Buddhists do not think of the Buddha as a god. They see him as an exceptional human being who came to understand the truth about life. He then spent the rest of his life teaching people how to achieve this for themselves. The Buddha said that people are reincarnated, or born again, after they die. This process of **reincarnation** ends when they live a good life in this world.

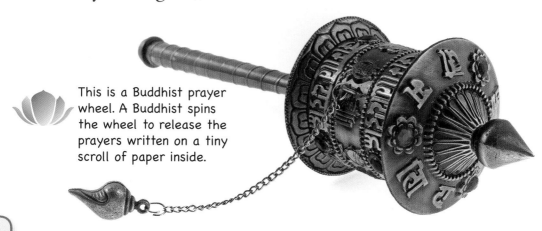

This is a Buddhist prayer wheel. A Buddhist spins the wheel to release the prayers written on a tiny scroll of paper inside.

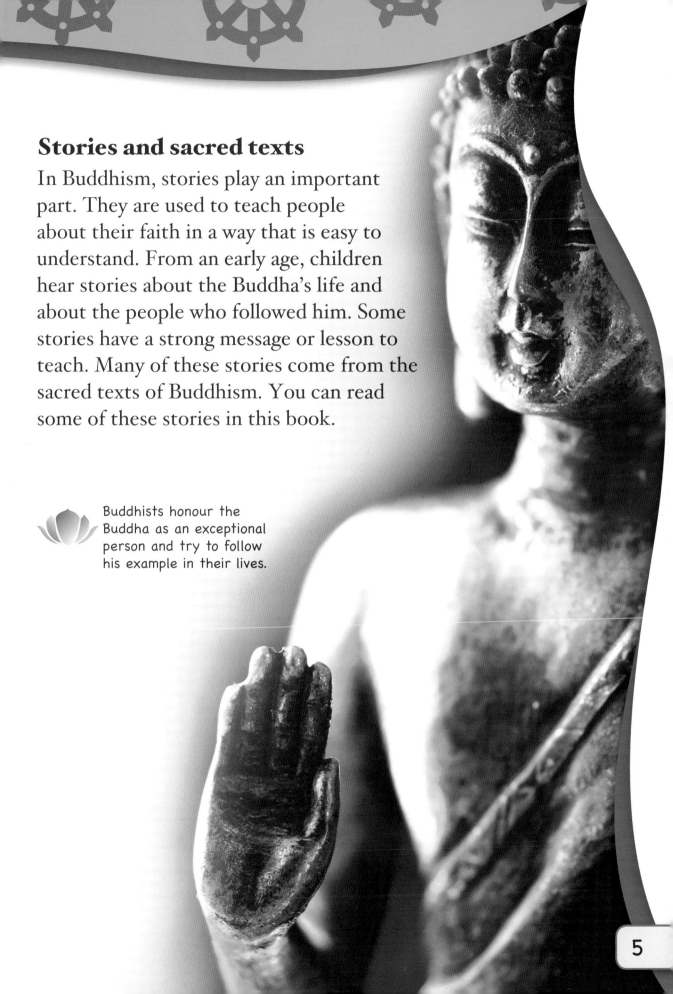

Stories and sacred texts

In Buddhism, stories play an important part. They are used to teach people about their faith in a way that is easy to understand. From an early age, children hear stories about the Buddha's life and about the people who followed him. Some stories have a strong message or lesson to teach. Many of these stories come from the sacred texts of Buddhism. You can read some of these stories in this book.

Buddhists honour the Buddha as an exceptional person and try to follow his example in their lives.

Siddhartha Grows Up

Hundreds of years ago, King Suddhodhana and his wife, Queen Maya, ruled over a mountain kingdom in northern India. They lived in splendid Kapilavastu, the capital of the kingdom.

One night, Queen Maya dreamed of a white elephant holding a lotus blossom in its trunk. She asked a wise man to tell her what the dream meant.

"This is wonderful news, your majesty," the wise man said. "You will have a son who will become a very great person indeed."

Soon afterwards, Queen Maya became pregnant. When it was almost time for her to have her baby, she set off for her father's home, as was the custom. On the way, she stopped to rest in a beautiful garden, and there, in the shade of a tree filled with blossom, her son was born.

Siddhartha was born in a garden in a place called Lumbini.

There was great rejoicing in Kapilavastu at the news of the baby's birth. He was named Siddhartha.

A few days later, an old man called Asita came to see the king. Asita was famous for his ability to see into the future. When he saw Siddhartha, he began to cry.

"Why are you crying, Asita?" asked the king. "What is wrong with our son?"

"Nothing is wrong, your majesty," the old man replied. "On the contrary. Your son is destined to become the greatest king in history, or the wisest teacher ever known. I am only sad because I am old and will not live to see this happen."

A week after Siddhartha's birth, Queen Maya died. Siddhartha was looked after by his aunt, Prajapati.

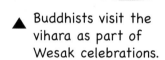

▲ Buddhists visit the vihara as part of Wesak celebrations.

Wesak Festival

Siddhartha is believed to have been born at the time of the full moon in May. On this day, many Buddhists also remember his **enlightenment** and death. They remember these three events at the festival of Wesak. This is a time for showing generosity, a very important Buddhist quality. People make offerings at the **vihara** (temple) and take gifts for the **monks**.

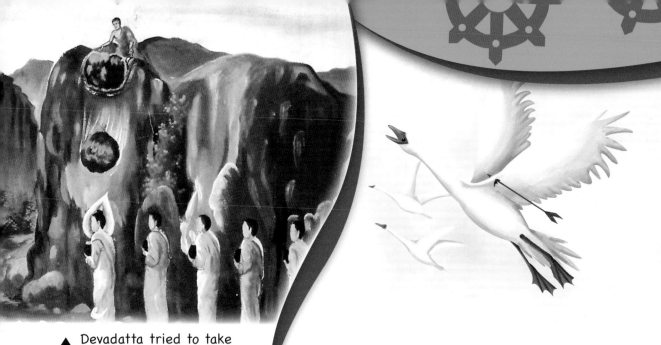

▲ Devadatta tried to take the Buddha's life on many different occasions.

Devadatta

When Siddhartha became the **Buddha**, his cousin, Devadatta, became one of his followers. Tradition says that Devadatta remained very jealous of his cousin, and tried to kill him several times. The plots failed but Devadatta caused a split among the Buddha's followers and set up his own **monastery**. Before he died, however, he was reunited with the Buddha.

Siddhartha grew up in his father's palace, surrounded by great luxury. He was tall, strong and handsome. Anyone who met him, loved him. At school, Siddhartha was a brilliant student. He quickly learned many subjects, including mathematics and languages. He became so good at his lessons that his teachers could not keep up with him.

King Suddhodhana wanted his son to become a great king. He made sure that Siddhartha learned all the skills that a king would need. So Siddhartha was taught how to use a bow and arrow, how to ride a horse and how to fight with a sword.

Even though Siddhartha became a skilful warrior, he was also caring and kind-hearted. He particularly loved the animals he saw around him in the palace grounds.

One day, Siddhartha was walking through the woods with his cousin, Devadatta. They looked up to see a flock of swans flying overhead. Before Siddhartha could stop him, Devadatta put an arrow into his bow, took aim and fired. Seconds later, one of the swans fell from the sky.

Both boys ran to where the swan had landed. Siddhartha reached it first, and found that the swan was still alive, but had Devadatta's arrow stuck in its wing. Gently, Siddhartha pulled the arrow out and wrapped the wound in leaves.

"That's my swan," shouted Devadatta, running up. "I shot it, so you'd better give it back to me!"

Siddhartha refused.

"I have saved the swan's life," he told Devadatta. "So it belongs to me."

One day, Siddhartha's cousin, Devadatta, shot and injured a swan with an arrow.

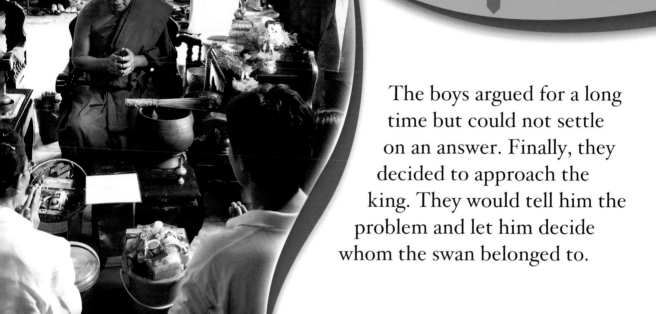

Followers of Buddhism follow the Five Precepts in their daily lives.

The boys argued for a long time but could not settle on an answer. Finally, they decided to approach the king. They would tell him the problem and let him decide whom the swan belonged to.

The Five Precepts

Buddhists follow a set of rules called the Five **Precepts.** They are:

1 Not to kill or harm living things
2 Not to take things that are not freely given
3 Not to have wrong relationships
4 Not to tell lies or speak unkindly
5 Not to drink alcohol or take drugs

Siddhartha looked after the swan until it was well. Then he took it to the woods and set it free.

The two boys entered the court with the swan. Quickly they told the king about what had happened in the woods.

"I shot the swan so it's mine," Devadatta informed the king.

"I saved the swan's life so it's mine," said Siddhartha.

The king and his ministers were puzzled. Whom did the swan belong to?

Just then, an old man appeared in the doorway. No one had ever seen him before.

"The swan belongs to the person who tried to save its life," the old man said. "Not to the person who tried to kill it."

"Thank you for your wise advice, old man," said the king. "Siddhartha can keep the swan."

So, Siddhartha looked after the swan until it was better. Then, he took it to the woods and let it fly away with its flock again.

Becoming the Buddha

Siddhartha grew up in great luxury. His father, King Suddhodhana, made sure that Siddhartha was protected from the world outside. The king was worried that, if Siddhartha saw people suffering, he might choose to become a great teacher instead of a king.

At the age of sixteen, Siddhartha married a beautiful princess called Yashodhara. In time, they had a son called Rahula. Siddhartha had everything he could possibly want. Yet, he was often unhappy.

King Suddhodhana made sure that Siddhartha had the best of everything.

One day, Siddhartha and his chariot driver, Channa, went for a drive in the countryside. Soon Siddhartha noticed a hunched-up old man by the roadside. Siddhartha asked Channa about the old man.

"He is just an old man," Channa replied. "Everyone gets old."

Next day, they passed a sick man.

"He is just a sick man," Channa explained. "Everyone gets sick."

The third time they rode out, they saw a corpse lying lifeless and still.

"He is dead," Channa told Siddhartha. "We all die one day."

The next day, they saw a **monk**.

"He looks so calm and peaceful," said Siddhartha.

"He is a holy man," replied Channa. "He has given up his home and belongings to search for true happiness."

"I shall be like him," thought Siddhartha.

The Three Jewels

Buddhists commit themselves to the Three Jewels:
1 The Buddha – as an ideal example to follow
2 The **Dharma** – or the Buddha's teachings
3 The **Sangha** – or the Buddhist community
They are called "jewels" because of their importance to Buddhists.

▼ Statues and paintings of the Buddha often show him meditating deeply.

The Bodhi Tree

The tree under which the Buddha gained **enlightenment** was a type of fig tree. It is called a **Bodhi** tree because bodhi means "enlightenment". It is an important symbol of Buddhism. The tree that stands in Bodh Gaya today is not the original tree. It is said that a cutting from the original was taken to Sri Lanka in the 3rd century BC, where it still grows.

▼ The Bodhi tree is an important symbol of the Buddhist religion.

That night, Siddhartha decided to leave his old life behind and try to find out why people suffered so much. At midnight, Siddhartha rode out of the palace with Channa. When he reached the river, he took off his fine clothes and put on a holy man's orange robes instead. Then he took his sword and cut off his long hair.

He told Channa to return to the palace and tell his family not to worry. One day, he would return to teach them what he had learned. Then he said goodbye.

Siddhartha began his search for a way to end the suffering he had seen. First, he joined two religious teachers and learned to meditate. Then, he spent six years in the forest with five other holy men. He lived a life of great hardship but still he did not find the answers he was looking for.

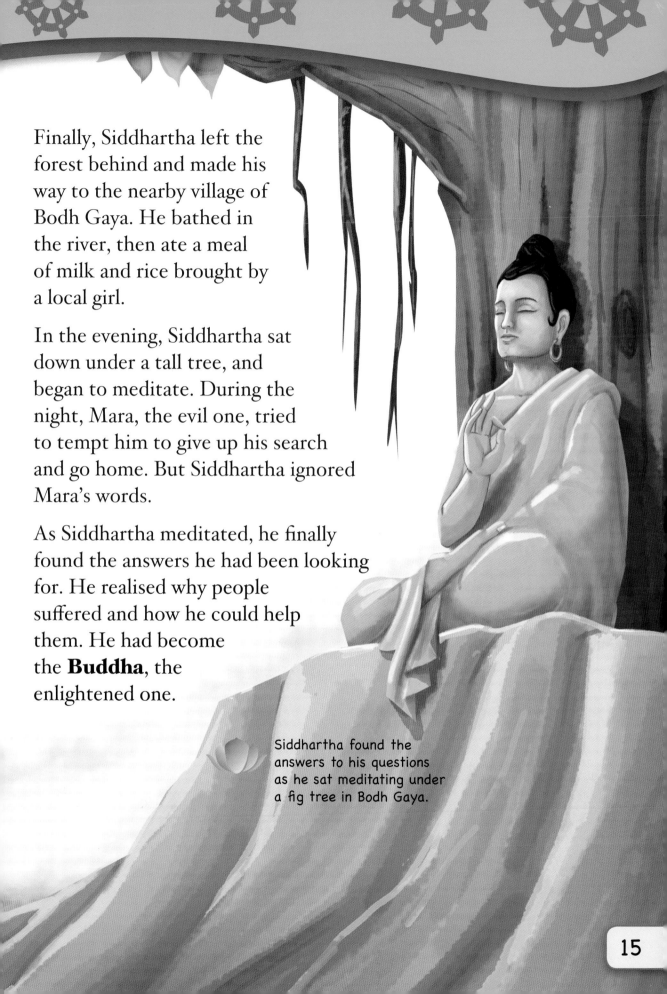

Finally, Siddhartha left the forest behind and made his way to the nearby village of Bodh Gaya. He bathed in the river, then ate a meal of milk and rice brought by a local girl.

In the evening, Siddhartha sat down under a tall tree, and began to meditate. During the night, Mara, the evil one, tried to tempt him to give up his search and go home. But Siddhartha ignored Mara's words.

As Siddhartha meditated, he finally found the answers he had been looking for. He realised why people suffered and how he could help them. He had become the **Buddha**, the enlightened one.

Siddhartha found the answers to his questions as he sat meditating under a fig tree in Bodh Gaya.

▲ This eight-spoked Dharma wheel symbolises the Noble Eightfold Path.

The Noble Eightfold Path

The Noble Eightfold Path showed people the way to live:

1 Understand the Buddha's teaching
2 Think about other people
3 Speak kindly and truthfully
4 Treat other people well
5 Earn your living by doing something that is not harmful
6 Work hard to do good things
7 Be calm and aware of your actions
8 Meditate to become calm and peaceful

Filled with great happiness, the Buddha meditated for many more days and nights. Two merchants brought him food and became his first followers. But he wanted to teach other people what he had learned. He travelled to a deer park near the holy city of Varanasi, and found the five holy men who had been his companions in the forest.

That evening the Buddha gave his first teaching to the holy men.

"The reason people suffer," he told them, "is because they are never happy with what they have got. They always want more. But there is a way to live so that everyone can find peace and happiness. That way is called the Noble Eightfold Path."

For the rest of his life, the Buddha travelled around India and taught people the right way to live. Many people came to hear him and became his followers.

When he was about 80 years old, the Buddha fell ill. Realising that his life was coming to an end, he called his monks together.

"My time with you is nearly over," he told them. "When I am gone, my teachings will guide you."

Then he made his last journey to the village of Kushinagara. Just outside the village, he stopped to rest in a **grove** of trees on the banks of a river. There he lay down between two trees and called for Ananda, his faithful friend.

"Do not be sad," the Buddha said. "Remember that nothing lasts for ever."

Then the Buddha passed away. But his teachings did not die with him. They are still followed, to this day, by millions of people all over the world.

The Buddha passed away peacefully surrounded by his followers.

Kisagotami and the Mustard Seed

Once, there was a young woman called Kisagotami. She came from a well-to-do family and was married to a rich merchant. In time, Kisagotami had a baby boy and was very happy. But when her son was about a year old, he fell ill and died before a doctor could be called.

Kisagotami was beside herself with grief. In her despair, she went from house to house, holding her child in her arms. She asked people if they knew of a medicine that would bring her son back to life. Some people took no notice of her. Others thought that she had gone mad.

Finally, she met a wise man who felt sorry for her loss.

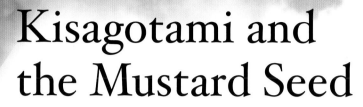

Kisagotami asked everyone how to bring her dead son back to life.

"You should go and see the **Buddha**," he said kindly. "He may be able to help."

At once, Kisagotami went to the local **monastery** where the Buddha was staying. Still cradling her child, she told the Buddha her sad story.

"He is my only son," she sobbed. "I beg you to help me bring him back to life."

The Buddha listened with great kindness and compassion to what Kisagotami said.

"Kisagotami," he said gently. "There is only one way to help you. You must go down into the town and bring me back a handful of mustard seeds."

"I can do that," replied Kisagotami.

"But," continued the Buddha, "you must only bring the mustard seeds from a house where no one has died."

Kisagotami felt very hopeful when she heard the Buddha's words. She set off immediately for the town.

The Metta Sutta

Kindness is a very important Buddhist quality. Buddhists call it **metta**. The **Metta Sutta** is a prayer about showing kindness.
"May all beings be happy,
May all beings be well,
Weak or strong,
Large or small,
Seen or unseen,
Here or elsewhere,
Present or to come,
In heights or depths,
May all beings be happy,
May all beings be well."

▼ Buddhist monks pray before a shrine in a monastery.

19

▲ Buddhists offer flowers at a shrine.

Offering Flowers

To show their respect for the Buddha, Buddhists place offerings of flowers at a **shrine**. The flowers remind people of the Buddha's teaching that everything is always changing. Nothing lasts for ever. Like everything else, the flowers eventually fade and die.

Hurrying into the town, Kisagotami stopped at the first house she saw.

"The Buddha has asked me to fetch some mustard seeds from a house where no one has died," she said.

"I'm sorry," came the answer. "But my mother and father died last year."

At the next house she visited, the answer was the same. And the next house. At every house in the town, somebody had died. By the end of the day, Kisagotami had collected no mustard seeds at all.

Then Kisagotami understood what it was that the Buddha wanted her to find out – that death touches everyone. Sadly, she took her son's body to be buried. Then she returned to the monastery.

The Buddha was waiting for Kisagotami.

"Have you brought the mustard seeds?" he asked her.

"No," replied Kisagotami. "And I won't try to find them anymore. I understand now what you were trying to teach me. I am not the only one who has lost a loved one."

"Yes," said the Buddha. "For everyone, death is a part of life. That is the only certainty."

After this, Kisagotami became a follower of the Buddha. She lived a very strict life and wore robes made out of rags.

The Buddha told Kisagotami that death touches everyone.

The Hungry Ghosts

Long ago, there lived a very holy man called Mu-lien, who followed the **Buddha** and became a **monk**. Before he left home to join the Buddha, Mu-lien had given his mother a large amount of money to give away to the monks who came to her door. But Mu-lien's mother was greedy.

Mu-lien's path was blocked by the bull-headed monsters of Hell.

She kept the money for herself and lied to Mu-lien when she saw him again. Because of this lie, she went to Hell when she died. Her punishment was to become a ghost who was always hungry but could never eat.

Kind Mu-lien felt sorry for his mother. He decided to try to save her, and set off for Hell to find her.

On the way, Mu-lien met Yama, the Lord of Hell.

"Your mother told a lie," said Yama. "And she must be punished. You can't save her now."

The judges who had sentenced his mother told him the same thing. But Mu-lien did not turn back. He continued his journey to the deepest, darkest part of Hell. Almost at once, Mu-lien's path was blocked by 50 dreadful, bull-headed monsters. Their eyes flashed red with flames.

Calmly, Mu-lien walked right past the beasts. The beasts could not harm him, since he was a holy man.

▲ Offerings of fruit and food are placed at a **shrine** during the Hungry Ghosts festival.

Hungry Ghosts Festival

Every year, in China, people celebrate the Festival of the Hungry Ghosts. It is believed that, on this day, the hungry ghosts leave Hell and wander the Earth in search of food. People also remember their dead ancestors on this day. They prepare a sumptuous feast for the "ghosts", hoping that this will bring them good luck in their lives.

▲ Children dancing during the O-bon festival in Japan.

O-bon Festival

O-bon is a Japanese festival which is very similar to the Festival of the Hungry Ghosts (see page 23). During the festival, people decorate their houses and light small bonfires to welcome home the spirits of their ancestors. At the end of the festival, they put miniature paper boats, filled with candles, on lakes and rivers to carry the spirits back to their world.

Eventually, Mu-lien reached the deepest part of Hell. He found his mother in a dark, dingy cell, tied to her bed by a rope so strong that no human being could break it.

"Help me, my son," pleaded his mother. "I have learned my lesson."

Mu-lien tried hard to untie the knots on the rope and free his mother. But no matter how hard he pulled, he could not loosen them.

In despair, Mu-lien went straight to see the Buddha, the only person with the power to help his mother.

"Lord Buddha, I beg you," said Mu-lien. "Please help my mother. I know she lied, but she does not deserve to suffer in this way.

"I promise you that in her next life on Earth, she will spend her time doing good deeds."

The Buddha smiled at Mu-lien.

"You are a good man, Mu-lien," he said. "You are kind and compassionate to everyone. I will help you and your mother."

Mu-lien bowed to the Buddha in thanks.

"There is just one condition," continued the Buddha. "Your mother must make up for her greed. So, every year, she should prepare a great feast for all of the monks. If she agrees to this, she can go free."

Of course, Mu-lien's mother agreed at once. Every year, as the Buddha had said, she cooked a great feast for the monks, using the best and finest ingredients that she could find. But she never forgot the hungry ghosts and always saved some of the food for them.

Every year Mu-lien's mother prepared a huge feast for the monks.

The Generous Prince

Prince Vessantara was famous for his generosity. Even as a young boy, he was always giving his belongings away.

When Vessantara was 16 years old, his father gave the kingdom to him to rule. Later, Vessantara married a beautiful princess, called Maddi, and had two children – a boy and a girl.

Prince Vessantara owned a white elephant. It was the most precious possession in the kingdom because it had the power to bring rain. At that time, a nearby kingdom was suffering from a terrible drought. In despair, the king sent eight of his priests to Vessantara to ask him for the elephant.

"You must take it," said Vessantara, handing the elephant over to them. "Your need is greater than mine."

The people of Vessantara's kingdom were furious that the elephant had been given away. They asked the old king to take charge again and banish his son from the kingdom. Reluctantly, the king agreed. Vessantara gave away all of his belongings. Then he and his family left in a chariot pulled by four fine horses.

Soon, they met a priest who asked for the horses. Vessantara gave them to him gladly. Next, they met a priest who asked for the chariot. Vessantara gave that away too.

The Prince and his family continued their journey on foot. Eventually, they reached a forest on the slopes of the Himalayan mountains. There, they lived in two small huts beside a lotus pond, eating only roots and fruits from the forest.

Prince Vessantara gave away his white elephant to the neighbouring kingdom.

▲ A scene from one of the Jataka stories painted on the walls of the Ajanta caves in India.

The Jatakas

The story of Prince Vessantara is called a **Jataka** story. The Jatakas are part of the Buddhist sacred texts, and tell of the Buddha's past lives. In them, the Buddha appears in human or animal form, to teach a particular quality, such as compassion or generosity. Of the hundreds of Jatakas, the Vessantara Jataka is the longest and most important.

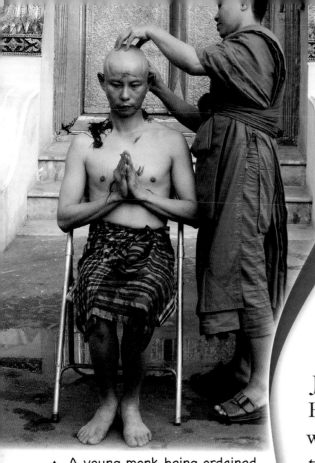

▲ A young monk being ordained during the Boun Pha Vet festival in Cambodia.

Boun Pha Vet Festival

The Boun Pha Vet Festival is celebrated in Laos in January. The festival honours Prince Vessantara and the Vessantara Jataka is read out. This is considered to be a good time for new monks to be **ordained**. The three-day festival is also celebrated with talks about the Buddha's life, fortune-telling, processions, dancing and plays.

In a nearby village, there lived a poor priest, called Jujaka, and his beautiful wife. Often she would be exhausted after doing her chores.

"I can't do this any longer," she told her husband. "You'll have to find me some servants."

Jujaka went to Prince Vessantara. He waited until Maddi was out of the way, then asked Vessantara for his two children to be his servants. Even though he loved his children dearly, Vessantara agreed to give them away.

Vessantara gave his children away to the priest Jujaka.

Some time later, another priest came by and asked Vessantara for his wife. Vessantara was heartbroken but still he agreed to give her away. Luckily, the priest was the god Indra in disguise.

"You are truly generous," he told Vessantara. "As a reward, I am giving you your wife back."

Meanwhile, Jujaka led Vessantara's children through the forest. Very soon, he was horribly lost. The gods slowly guided his footsteps to the king's palace.

The king was overjoyed to see his grandchildren again. The children told him that their parents were alive and well.

"But you didn't love our father," they said. "Or you wouldn't have sent him away."

Without further delay, the king set out to find Vessantara and Maddi, and bring them home.

When Vessantara saw his father and children, he could hardly believe his eyes. Weeping with joy, they were reunited.

The family went back to the palace. Vessantara was crowned king and ruled wisely for many years.

Finally, Vessantara was reunited with his children and lived happily.

Glossary

bodhi – enlightenment, having all the knowledge

Buddha – the enlightened one

Dharma – the teachings of the Buddha that Buddhists use as a guide to living their lives

enlightenment – a state when a person knows the answers to the problems of life

grove – garden full of trees

Jataka – Buddhist sacred texts that tell of the Buddha's past lives

Metta Sutta – the Buddhist prayer about showing loving kindness

metta – the quality of loving kindness

monastery – place where monks live and worship

monk – holy man

ordain – select or appoint someone as a monk in a monastery

precept – direction given as a code of conduct

reincarnation – rebirth of the soul in a new body

sangha – the Buddhist community

shrine – place where people go to honour a holy person and pray

vihara – Buddhist temple

Find out more

Websites

http://www.geocities.com/Tokyo/Courtyard/1652/Story.html
A great collection of stories about Buddhism.

http://www.serve.com/cmtan/buddhism/Stories/
Another collection of stories about Buddhism for children and parents.

http://www.buddhanet.org/
A website giving information on a wide range of Buddhist topics.

Books

21st Century Religions: Buddhism by Anita Ganeri
Publisher: Wayland, 2005

Atlas of World Faiths: Buddhism by Anita Ganeri
Publisher: Franklin Watts 2007

Jatakamala: Stories from the Buddha's Previous Births by A.N.D. Haksar (Translator)
Publisher: HarperCollins, 2003

Stories from Buddhist Lands by S. Dhammika and Susan Harmer
Publisher: Times Editions, Marshall Cavendish, 2005

Index